THE HISPANIC INFLUENCE IN THE UNITED STATES

LATINOS
IN AMERICAN HISTORY

FRANCISCO VASQUEZ DE CORONADO

BY JIM WHITING

P.O. Box 619
Bear, Delaware 19701

THE HISPANIC INFLUENCE IN THE UNITED STATES

LATINOS
IN AMERICAN HISTORY

OTHER TITLES IN THE SERIES

Visit us on the web: www.mitchelllane.com
Comments? email us: mitchelllane@mitchelllane.com

THE HISPANIC INFLUENCE IN THE UNITED STATES

LATINOS
IN AMERICAN HISTORY

FRANCISCO VASQUEZ DE
CORONADO

BY JIM WHITING

Mitchell Lane
PUBLISHERS

First Printing

Library of Congress Cataloging-in-Publication Data

Whiting, Jim, 1943-
      Francisco Vasquez de Coronado/Jim Whiting.
         p. cm. — (Latinos in American history)
      Summary: Discusses the life and exploration of the Spanish nobleman, Francisco Vasquez de Coronado.
      Includes bibliographical references (p.) and index.
      ISBN 1-58415-146-3 (lib bdg.)
      1. Coronado, Francisco Vásquez de, 1510-1554—Juvenile literature. 2. Explorers—America—Biography—Juvenile literature. 3. Explorers—Spain—Biography—Juvenile literature. 4. America—Discovery and exploration—Spanish—Juvenile literature. 5. Southwest, New—Discovery and exploration—Spanish—Juvenile literature. [1. Coronado, Francisco Vásquez de, 1510-1544. 2. Explorers. 3. Southwest, New—Discovery and exploration. 4. America—Discovery and exploration—Spanish.] I. Title. II. Series.
      E125.V3 W48 2002   2002022143

ABOUT THE AUTHOR: Jim Whiting has been a journalist, writer, editor, and photographer for more than 20 years. In addition to a lengthy stint as publisher of *Northwest Runner* magazine, Mr. Whiting has contributed to the *Seattle Times*, *Conde Nast Traveler*, *Newsday*, and *Saturday Evening Post*. He has edited more than 20 titles in the Mitchell Lane Real-Life Reader Biography series and Unlocking the Secrets of Science. He lives in Washington state with his wife and two teenage sons.

PHOTO CREDITS: Cover: Corbis; p. 6 Superstock; p. 10 Getty Images; p. 14 Corbis; p. 17 Corbis; p. 18 Corbis; p. 20 B. Marvis; p. 26 Northwind Photos; p. 28 Getty Images; pp. 31, 34 B. Marvis; p. 37 Corbis; p. 39 Northwind Photos; p. 40 B. Marvis; p. 44 B. Marvis; p. 46 Northwind Photos

PUBLISHER'S NOTE: This story is based on the author's extensive research, which he/she believes to be accurate. Some parts of the text might have been created by the author based on his/her research to illustrate what might have happened years ago, and is solely an aid to readability for young adults.

      The spelling of the names in this book follow the generally accepted usage of modern day. The spelling of Spanish names in English has evolved over time with no consistency. Many names have been anglicized and no longer use the accent marks or any Spanish grammar. Others have retained the Spanish grammar. Hence, we refer to Hernando de Soto as "de Soto," but Francisco Vásquez de Coronado as "Coronado." There are other variances as well. Some sources might spell Vásquez as Vázquez. For the most part, we have adapted the more widely recognized spellings.

CONTENTS

Coronado's march (1540-42) in search of the golden wealth of the fabulous "Seven Cities of Cibola" was the first expedition to penetrate the Central West of the United States. Traveling from the Mexican border through Taos, New Mexico and Western Texas, his army pushed as far as the site of Great Bend, Kansas.

GOLD, GOD AND GLORY

The ancient Greeks invented stories about a creature called a chimera. It was an animal with the head of a lion, the body of a goat, and the tail of a snake. For good measure, it spit fire like a dragon.

Did such an animal exist? Of course not. It was purely imaginary. In modern-day English, a chimera is something that is an illusion, something that is not real. It exists only in a person's imagination.

But there was nothing imaginary about the vast riches that Spain began taking from the New World within a few years following Columbus' voyage to the New World. In less than 50 years, Spanish conquistadores leading relatively small bands of well-armed men had conquered huge territories in Central and South America. This newfound wealth had enabled Spain to become the most powerful nation on earth. It was an exciting and glorious time to be a Spaniard.

At the same time, the Spanish also believed it was their duty to introduce the Christian religion to the native peoples in the regions they conquered. If Spain in the early 16th century had had a national motto, it would have been Gold, God, and Glory.

So it wasn't surprising that on February 22, 1540—exactly 192 years before George Washington was born—a Spanish nobleman named Francisco Vásquez de Coronado was looking forward to a very bright future. Just three days away from celebrating his 30th birthday, he had already enjoyed a spectacular rise to power since his arrival in the New World less than five years earlier.

The scene was the town of Compostela in Mexico, several hundred miles south of present-day Arizona's border. Coronado was in command of an expedition that was preparing to leave the next morning. All around him was the clinking of armor, the shouting of men, the lowing and bleating of hundreds of cattle and sheep, sounds of last-minute packing, and all the chaos and disorder of well over a thousand people starting out on a long trip.

Coronado had invested a lot of his own money to help outfit this expedition—more than a million dollars in today's money, in fact. But he thought it was a good investment. He felt sure that within a few months he would return to Compostela, then go on to the capital, Mexico City, with enough gold to repay his original investment several times over. The men who would go with him were excited, too. They believed that they would make enough money to live in comfort and style for the rest of their lives.

All this activity and excitement had its origins many years earlier. About the year 700, the Moors of North Africa, who were believers in the religion of Islam, crossed into Christian Spain and conquered it. In most cases the Moors did not persecute the Spaniards for their religion, but the Spaniards resented the fact that their country was ruled by foreigners—especially foreigners who were not Christian.

About the year 1,000—at roughly the same time that intrepid Vikings from Iceland were crossing the frigid North Atlantic Ocean to discover the North American continent—a legend arose. According to this legend, seven Spanish bishops and their congregations sailed west to escape their Muslim conquerors. When they landed, they founded seven cities close together. These cities soon prospered and became very wealthy.

In the meantime, native Spaniards fought the Moors and began to win back portions of their country, a little at a time. This process ended in 1492, when the last remaining Moors were driven from the city of Granada. A few months later, Christopher Columbus sailed west and discovered the New World. Other Spanish adventurers soon followed him, and it didn't take long before they began returning to their native country with huge amounts of gold and silver.

Soon legend and reality became combined. The seven cities that the bishops had supposedly founded became known as the Seven Cities of Gold. It was believed that whoever discovered them would become fabulously wealthy.

This belief was so strong that an expedition of 400 men under the command of Pánfilo de Narváez left Spain in 1527. They landed in Florida the following year and planned to proceed westward along the coast of the Gulf of Mexico, then go ashore to search for the seven cities on horseback and on foot. They vanished without a trace.

Two years later, a Spaniard named Nuñez de Guzmán, who had lived in Mexico for several years, began to hear stories about seven cities with streets paved with gold. These cities lay far to the north of Mexico. He headed in that direction with a few soldiers to investigate, but soon found an easier way of making money. He would capture Indians, then sell them as slaves, even though the Spanish government had expressly forbidden the taking of slaves. The reality was, however, that the Spanish landowners living in Mexico did not want to do hard work. The only way to mine the gold and silver that were making Spain so rich was through cruelly hard work. At the time, slavery seemed to be the best answer.

For several years, Guzmán made good money capturing slaves. In 1536 he was on yet another slave-hunting expedition when something astonishing happened. He found four men who were the only survivors of the Narváez expedition.

Many explorers tried to find the legendary "Seven Cities of Gold." Álvar Nuñez Cabeza de Vaca, illustrated here, claimed to be one of four survivors of an expedition led by Pánfilo de Narváez.

They had traveled back and forth for eight years with different Indian tribes, who for the most part had treated them kindly because they had become healers.

Guzmán brought the four men back to Mexico City, where they were welcomed as great heroes. The viceroy, or ruler—a man named Antonio de Mendoza—eagerly questioned them. Like everyone else, Mendoza had heard about the seven cities of gold. He knew that if he could find them and bring back the treasure, he would become famous and a great favorite of the king of Spain.

But the leader of the little group, Álvar Cabeza de Vaca, told Mendoza the truth. All he had seen in eight years of wandering was empty lands. "They were remote and malign, devoid of resources," he said.

The viceroy pressed him. "But surely there is more," he insisted.

Cabeza de Vaca thought for a moment. Then he told Mendoza of something that he had heard but not seen himself. One of the Indian tribes he had spent time with had spoken of another tribe, far away to the north. This second tribe lived in large houses in great cities. But more important, at least to Mendoza's eager ears, these Indians appeared to be very wealthy. They had much turquoise and emeralds, Cabeza de Vaca had been told.

Even though this story did not include any mention of gold, it was all the encouragement Mendoza needed. His imagination did the rest. He decided to organize a large expedition to travel north and find those cities. Because it would take a long time to put together such a large expedition, he preceded it with a much smaller group led by Marcos de Niza, a friar of the Catholic Church, called Fray Marcos. (*Fray*, pronounced *fry*, is Spanish for *friar*.). They left in February 1539. Accompanying that group was

Esteban, also called Estevanico, a black man who had been one of the four survivors.

Esteban was very full of himself. He wore long flowing bright-colored robes and carried a decorated gourd that the Indians had given him during his earlier travels. The gourd seemed to have magical powers—indeed, it was the symbol of a medicine man—and Esteban felt that it would guarantee him a very warm welcome each time he visited a new tribe.

Fray Marcos soon sent Esteban on ahead with some Indians to help carry baggage. He instructed Esteban to send back a cross whenever he discovered a new Indian city. The larger the cross, the larger the city.

Not long afterward, an Indian returned to Fray Marcos, staggering under the weight of a huge cross. Esteban had learned of seven very large cities that were still far to the north. Together, they were known as Cibola.

Fray Marcos was very excited. He pushed on in Esteban's path, which was easy to follow. A steady flow of messengers came back, each one bearing tales of still greater riches.

But without warning, the news suddenly turned grim. Two Indians, both wounded, staggered into camp. Esteban and everyone with him had been killed as they approached the first city of Cibola.

Determined to find the riches, Fray Marcos continued on until he saw what he believed was the first city of Cibola far in the distance. He believed he saw the walls gleaming with precious metals. Some people believe that what he saw may just have been the reflection of the setting sun. Others say that he was so blinded by the desire to see gold that he saw what he wanted to see.

Fray Marcos didn't go any closer to investigate, because his main responsibility was to return and report what he had found to the viceroy. He didn't want to end up the way that Esteban had.

By the time he returned to Mexico City, six months after he left, Fray Marcos was full of tales about the richness of what lay ahead. The Seven Cities of Cibola inflamed everyone's imagination. There was no shortage of volunteers for the expedition that would shortly follow, as there seemed to be enough gold and glory for everyone. And several friars, including Fray Marcos, would go along to make sure that God was included as well.

In February 1540, Coronado and his one thousand men set off in a slow-moving cloud of dust. They didn't know it, but they were pursuing a chimera.■

As Coronado came across villages and towns in his quest for the "Seven Cities of Gold," he erected a wooden cross at various locations to mark the area his men had been to.

FRANCISCO VASQUEZ DE CORONADO

Francisco Vásquez de Coronado was born on February 25, 1510, in the Spanish city of Salamanca. His parents, Juan Vásquez de Coronado and Isabel de Lujan, were wealthy aristocrats who owned a large estate. Because of their wealth and social position, they would have been well-known at the court of King Ferdinand and Queen Isabella.

Francisco was his parents' second son. He romped and played with his siblings in the family house, had plenty of servants to wait upon him, and received the best possible education. But as he grew older he became aware that his older brother would inherit the family estate. While he would never have to worry about living in poverty, when he was an adult he would have to leave his fine home and live somewhere else. He wouldn't have much money, and probably just a servant or two to make his life a little easier.

Or he could try to make his own fortune.

When he was nine years old, an event happened that would have a profound influence on the way that his life turned out, although he hardly realized it at the time.

A Spanish conquistador named Hernán Cortés landed on the eastern coast of Mexico with a force of several hundred men. Amazingly, he soon penetrated into the heart of Mexico to the ancient Aztec capital of Tenochtitlán and defeated an army many times his size. He claimed the entire Aztec empire in the name of Spain. Other explorers such as Francisco Pizarro, who conquered the Inca Empire in Peru, soon followed him. Within two decades Spain had acquired a huge empire.

But an empire that size needed a government. Though Cortés wanted to be governor of Mexico, he had made enemies at the Spanish court. They were suspicious that if he became governor, he would be more interested in doing what was best for him, not what was best for Spain.

So the Spanish king, Charles I, decided to appoint someone else. Three men turned him down. His fourth choice, Antonio de Mendoza, would determine the course of Coronado's life.

Born in 1490, Mendoza was a distant relative of the king. He had previously served as the Spanish ambassador to Rome. Like the Coronados, his family had spent a lot of time at the Spanish court, where Mendoza must have met the young Francisco and acted as a sort of mentor to him. When Mendoza departed for his new position, he invited the young man to accompany him.

Francisco probably did not hesitate to accept. He was 25, in the prime of life, and eager to make his mark on the world. Unless something happened to his older brother, his

prospects at home were very limited. So he followed
Mendoza to Mexico City, which had been built on the ruins
of the Aztec capital and was already a bustling town. He
began serving in responsible positions, which confirmed
Mendoza's judgment in bringing him along. He proved to be
loyal, very efficient, and totally honest. Soon Mendoza gave
him a seat on the town council of Mexico City.

*Hérnan Cortés, illustrated here on horseback, landed on the eastern coast of Mexico with
several hundred men and claimed the entire area in the name of Spain.*

Mendoza wasn't the only older man Francisco impressed. Alonso de Estrada, who was the illegitimate son of King Ferdinand, had been in Mexico for several years. During that time, he became treasurer of the region and one of its richest men. He took note of the young man's prospects, and within two years of his arrival, Francisco had married Alonso's daughter Beatriz. She was six years younger than her new husband and, like him, had been born in Spain.

There was no shortage of volunteers to set out from Mexico in search of the gold. Even Hernán Cortés wanted to take charge of the expedition, but he had long since fallen out of favor.

Coronado continued to impress those around him. Soon after his marriage, he was ordered to break up a rebellion at a nearby silver mine. A group of Indians and black slaves had taken it over. Coronado put down the uprising with a minimum of casualties.

That led to his next promotion. Mendoza named Coronado to be the governor of New Galicia, a province located to the northwest of Mexico City. Coronado set off with his wife and set up their new home in Compostela, which was the province's capital.

Soon afterward, Fray Marcos arrived in Mexico City with his electrifying news. Mendoza decided to send out a full-scale expedition to bring back the gold that he was sure lay waiting to be plundered. Although he briefly considered leading the expedition himself, he realized that he had to stay behind to administer the country for the king.

There was no shortage of volunteers to lead the expedition. Even Cortés himself wanted to take charge. But he had long since fallen from favor. Few people trusted him.

As soon as Mendoza decided that he wouldn't personally lead the ambitious expedition to the Seven Cities of Cibola, convert the Indians who lived in the region to Christianity, and bring glory to everyone, he almost certainly had someone else in mind. Someone who was loyal, trustworthy, brave, and competent. That someone was Francisco Vásquez de Coronado.■

This expanse in Arizona photographed in 1996 doesn't look very different from when Coronado's men passed through it more than 450 years earlier.

ON TO CIBOLA

Viceroy Mendoza must have been proud of what he saw pass in review before him. Several centuries of fighting the Moors had toughened Spanish soldiers, making them among the world's most skillful warriors. Many of the men in the review, their armor glinting in the sun, were sons of the finest families in Spain. Like Coronado, they had come to the New World because they had older brothers who would inherit the family estates. They carried the most modern weapons, including lances, crossbows, muskets, and keen-edged swords made of sturdy steel.

Like Coronado, Mendoza had also put a lot of his own money into the expedition. As he watched the splendid men who were about to head north, he must have felt confident that he had made a good investment.

As each man passed by, the viceroy ordered him to go to an inspector, who wrote down the man's name and a list of his possessions. Those records still survive, so we know the names of the men who went on the expedition and what each of them brought with him.

Coronado, for example, had 23 horses and four suits of armor.

Coronado's second in command, Lope de Samaniego, brought along 16 horses, two buckskin jackets, a coat of mail, cuirasses, and "arms of the country" (weapons made by local Indians such as bows and arrows).

On the other hand, a man named Juan de Vegara had only his mule.

Another member of the expedition was a soldier named Pedro de Castañeda. He later wrote an account of the expedition that provides us with many details.

Counting a few men who had gone ahead, Coronado had 336 soldiers under his command. Most of them were horsemen, but a few dozen were infantrymen who marched on foot. While nearly all of the expedition members were Spaniards, there were a handful of Portuguese, two Italians, a Frenchman, and a German. There was also a Scot named Thomas Blake; he appears on the records as Tomás Blaque. There were also Fray Marcos, four other friars, and three women—a nurse and the wives of two of the men.

The inspector, however, did not consider it necessary to write down the names of any of the Indians who went on the trip. Nearly a thousand went along to carry baggage and take care of the hundreds of animals—horses that weren't being ridden, as well as cattle and sheep for food.

Because the review took so long, the expedition didn't push off until the next day. And once it got going, a group that large couldn't move very fast. Having so many animals to keep track of and feed made progress even slower. The men on foot had no trouble keeping up with the horsemen.

The first part of the trip must have been enjoyable. The country was fertile, and adventurous Spanish settlers had already established homesteads, many of them with gardens.

The expedition paused at the village of Chiametla, some 200 miles from the starting point. One of Coronado's trusted lieutenants, Melchior Díaz, had departed several months previously on a scouting expedition. He met the army at Chiametla, and his news was not good. Several Indians who had accompanied him had died from exposure to the cold weather, and he hadn't seen anything that remotely resembled the wealthy villages that Fray Marcos had claimed to see. His report may have caused Coronado to have some doubts about the expedition's success, but it was too late to stop even if he had wanted to.

That wasn't the only bad thing that happened at Chiametla. While he was out looking for food for the army, de Samaniego was killed when an Indian shot an arrow into his eye. He hadn't had much time to use all the equipment he had brought along.

By April 1, the expedition had covered only 300 miles as it arrived at the village of Culiacán. That was far too slow a pace. Coronado took about 100 of the best men with him and left the rest of the expedition to wait until further orders. For several weeks, this advance party traveled through fertile lands near the Gulf of California. But as they moved into what is now Arizona, the landscape turned more rugged. The Spaniards called this barren area the *despoblado*, or "desolate wilderness." There was almost no food.

Soon afterward, Coronado arrived at a village called Chichilticalli. Fray Marcos had told them that it was an important town with several thousand people. It turned out to be something a little different. It was a single mud hut. And there was no food. The starving men had no choice but to keep going.

Yet an even worse shock awaited them. On the night of July 6, the adventurers made their camp. Just over a hill lay Hawikuh, the first of the Seven Cities of Cibola. All the hardships of the expedition were over, they thought. Soon they would be among the gilded streets of the wealthy city.

The next morning, as they drew over the hill and onto a broad plain, they soon realized that they had been deceived. Hawikuh was a pueblo, a collection of stone houses surrounded by an adobe wall. There was no evidence of gold or silver.

However, Coronado knew that Hawikuh had something that at that moment was more important than precious metal: food.

In a letter written soon afterward to Mendoza that described what had happened since the expedition began, Coronado explained his plight as he looked at Hawikuh: "We were in such great need of food that I thought we should all die of hunger if we continued to be without provisions for another day, since altogether we did not have two bushels of corn, and so I was obliged to hasten forward without delay."

Standing between him and the food, however, was a band of armed Zuni Indians drawn up on the plain in front of the city.

According to Spanish law, Coronado had to read them the *requerimiento*, or "requirement." That was a document that all Spanish commanders read to native peoples in the Americas. Under its terms, the natives would immediately become Spanish subjects and had to accept the beliefs of Christianity.

The Zunis were not impressed. They began firing arrows. One pierced the flowing gown of one of the priests standing near Coronado.

Coronado faced a dilemma. Under his orders, he was to conquer the new territory without killing anyone. He urged his men to remain calm.

But, as his letter to Mendoza revealed, "When the Indians saw that we did not move, they took greater courage, and grew so bold that they came up almost to the heels of our horses to shoot their arrows. On this account I saw that it was no longer time to hesitate, and as the priests approved the action, I charged them."

They shouted the traditional Spanish battle cry, "*Santiago y a ellos!*" which means "St. James [a patron saint of Spain] and at them!" Then the little army surged forward.

The Spaniards killed a few Indians, and the rest took flight back inside the walls of the pueblo. They gave no evidence that they would open the gates to feed Coronado's starving men. Coronado ordered his army to continue the attack.

At first things didn't go well for the invaders.

"The crossbowmen broke all the strings of their crossbows and the musketeers could do nothing, because they had arrived so weak and feeble that they could scarcely stand on their feet," Coronado said in his letter.

In addition, it was obvious to the people of Hawikuh that Coronado was the leader of the attackers. He had read the *requerimiento* to them, and his gilded armor, brighter than what the other men wore, gleamed in the sun. So they directed many of their arrows and rocks at him. Even though he was wearing a helmet, he was struck by several rocks and fell to the ground, unconscious. He had to be dragged to safety.

However, Coronado's men fought hard and the Zuni Indians couldn't stand up to them. Soon the Zunis surrendered. That surrender ended the first real military battle between Europeans and natives in what would one day become the United States of America. Those battles would continue for more than 350 years.

While none of Coronado's men died, several suffered arrow wounds and three horses were killed. The Spanish

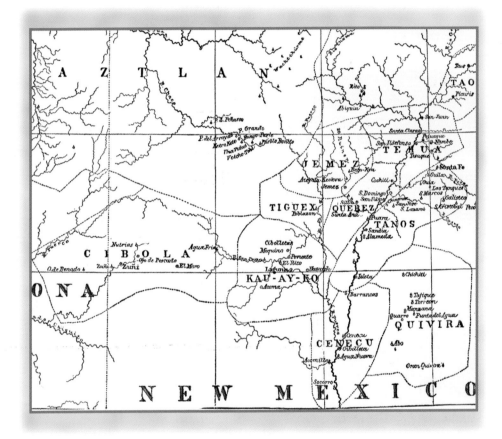

This map of the Pueblo region in New Mexico and Arizona shows the approximate location of many of the villages and towns that Coronado and his men passed through.

raided the granaries and soon ate their fill. Once they had met their objective, they were in no hurry to depart.

Several weeks later, Coronado wrote his long letter to Mendoza. He described what had happened so far and explained that they hadn't found any riches. He sent Fray Marcos back with the team of horsemen that would deliver the bad news to the viceroy. He felt sure that the friar's life would be in danger if he remained, because everyone in the army was so mad at him. The soldiers believed that Fray Marcos had lied to them.

"I can assure your Lordship that in reality, he has not told the truth in a single thing that he has said, but everything is the reverse of what he has said," Coronado wrote.

Then, in the midst of a long description of how the people of Cibola lived, he dropped the bad news: "As far as I can judge, it does not appear to me that there is any hope of getting gold or silver, but I trust in God that, if there is any, we shall get our share of it, and it shall not escape us through any lack of diligence in the search."

During the weeks that they spent at Hawikuh, Coronado and his men observed the way the people lived. Though they weren't rich, they seemed to be at peace. Also, a change seemed to come over Coronado. While he was bitterly disappointed that he had found no gold, he thought that perhaps he could explore the surrounding territory to see if it held anything else worthwhile. He sent four of his trusted lieutenants out into the wilderness with smaller parties.

Taken together, these four expeditions would uncover vast territories and remain one of the enduring legacies of Coronado's expedition. But one of them would also cast a permanent stain on his good name.■

As Coronado heard reports of riches throughout the region, he sent various expeditions made up of his most trusted men. Each expedition discovered much of the natural beauty of the western United States, but the men never found the gold they were searching for.

FOUR

EXPLORATIONS OF DISCOVERY

Coronado had heard reports that a kingdom called Tusayan, made up of seven villages, lay a few days to the northwest. There was that magic number seven again. Maybe these were the seven golden cities. In late July, Coronado sent Pedro de Tovar and about 20 men to investigate.

Early in his journey, Tovar discovered what is now known as the Painted Desert. Purple, gray, and red rocks lay all over the landscape, and their colors change hourly according to the position of the sun.

Tovar pushed on and soon arrived at the first city, a pueblo occupied by Hopi Indians. After a brief skirmish, the fighting stopped and the Spanish were showered with gifts. The scene was repeated at several other Hopi villages, but none of them had any precious metals. Tovar, however, did learn one thing from the Indians: There was a "great river" that lay farther west.

Tovar quickly returned to Coronado and gave his report. Coronado was excited. At that time, no one knew how truly wide the American continent was. Some people believed there was a water passage from the Atlantic to the Pacific. Maybe this river that the Indians had spoken of was that water passage. If it was, its discovery might make up for not finding gold at Cibola. Coronado sent out a second expedition of about two dozen horsemen under the command of García López de Cárdenas.

López de Cárdenas and his men quickly reached Tusayan, then pressed farther west. Three weeks later, they stood on the edge of one of the planet's great natural wonders, the Grand Canyon. Far below them lay the Colorado River, which from their high elevation seemed like a tiny little brook. Far across on the horizon lay the massive Colorado Plateau, which now contains the greatest concentration of national parks in the entire United States.

However, the Spaniards were not impressed with the natural beauty that today attracts tens of thousands of tourists annually. They were hungry and thirsty, and the region seemed cold and hostile. They sent their three best climbers to try to reach the river, which lay a mile beneath them in a chasm carved over uncounted millions of years. But the men couldn't even get close and had to turn back. Worse, the rugged terrain made it impossible to follow the river to its mouth. Cárdenas led his men back to Hawikuh.

The third exploration was under the command of Melchior Díaz, who was one of the most remarkable members of the entire expedition. He was the only leader who wasn't of noble birth. He had risen to be the *alcalde*, or mayor, of the frontier city of Culiacán and other posts because of his natural ability.

Díaz began his exploration for Coronado—by far the longest of the four—by heading south along the route that

López de Cárdenas and his men were the first Europeans to discover the Grand Canyon. Formed over a period of about a million years, the gorge you see in both photos was created by the Colorado River.

Coronado had traveled to reach Hawikuh. He encountered the main body of the expedition and ordered them forward to join Coronado at Hawikuh. After that, he headed west to try to meet a group of ships carrying additional supplies. He traveled over a hot, barren, lifeless desert that later explorers would call Camino del Diablo, or Devil's Highway. After 300 miles, he found the Colorado River, which López de Cárdenas had seen several hundred miles upstream. He also learned that three Spanish supply ships had sailed up it several weeks earlier, but had had to leave.

Díaz and his men rode north along the eastern bank of the river, then crossed into what is now California. They found even more inhospitable terrain—barren sand dunes, beds of burning lava, boiling springs—at the southern end of what is now known as the Imperial Valley, part of the Colorado Desert. The expedition had to turn back.

Díaz himself came to an unfortunate end not long afterward. He had brought along a flock of sheep to help feed his men. One day a greyhound that was accompanying the expedition began chasing some of the sheep. Perhaps frustrated by all the hardships of his journey, Díaz rode after the dog and threw his long lance at it. The lance missed and stuck in the sand. With his horse galloping at full speed, Díaz rammed into the butt end. The blow caused severe internal injuries that resulted in his death a few days later.

The fourth expedition originated when two strange Indians appeared at Hawikuh. Even though they lived more than 200 miles to the east, they had heard of Coronado and his expedition and wished to meet him. One of the Indians was quickly named Bigotes, which is Spanish for "mustache." Though most Indians had no facial hair, Bigotes had a huge set of whiskers. The two Indians told Coronado that they lived by a great river and lived off "great cattle" that roamed in massive herds on the open plains near their homes. A party of 20 horsemen under the command of Hernando de Alvarado headed east, guided by Bigotes.

He led the small group into a fertile valley on the upper Rio Grande. It was known as Tiguex, which so impressed Alvarado that he wrote a letter to Coronado urging him to bring the rest of the army and spend the winter there.

Alvarado pressed on. He arrived at a large pueblo called Cicuye, where he met an Indian whose tribe lived far to the east. He had been captured and made a slave. The Spaniards called him the Turk, because he resembled someone from Turkey, a country at the other end of the Mediterranean Sea from Spain. The Turk guided them even farther east, where Alvarado and his party became the first Spaniards to see these "great cattle," which were actually buffalo. The buffalo appeared in such profusion that the amazed Spaniards could only compare them with the fishes in the sea. The Spaniards also acquired a healthy respect for the bulls, which killed several of their horses with their sharp horns when the men rode too close.

But their amazement over the buffalo herds was soon overshadowed by stories of amazing riches that lay far beyond the horizon.■

Barren and parched, much of the land that Coronado and his men traveled over was difficult terrain. There were broad and barren deserts with scorpions, cactus, and steep mountains. As winter approached, the men had to set up camp and they raided several Native American villages to provide them with blankets and clothing.

TROUBLE AT TIGUEX

It hadn't taken much to persuade Coronado to follow Alvarado's advice. With the bulk of his expedition scheduled to arrive soon, the resources of the countryside around Hawikuh, which was barren and parched, would be stretched to the limit and perhaps even beyond. Coronado made preparations to follow his lieutenant to the east and sent word to the slowly approaching men to join him there.

So far he had done an excellent job of following his orders, in particular the part that he was to treat the Indians kindly. But that was about to change.

Part of the trouble began when the Turk told Alvarado about Quivira, his original home to the east. "It is rich with gold," the Turk said. "You would need wagons to haul it away." Quivira soon had the magical reputation that Cibola had enjoyed less than a year before.

Alvarado's greed was quickly rekindled. But he was suspicious, especially since he'd already been disappointed. "If gold is as plentiful as you say," he said to the Turk, "why aren't you wearing any?"

The Turk replied that when he was captured, he had been wearing a gold bracelet, but Bigotes had taken it.

Alvarado hurried back to Cicuye and confronted Bigotes.

"Where is the bracelet you took from the Turk?" he demanded.

"The man is a liar," Bigotes answered. "There never was such a bracelet."

Alvarado refused to believe Bigotes. First the Spaniard set vicious dogs on him. Then he put the unfortunate man into chains and dragged him back to Tiguex. That was extremely ungrateful on Alvarado's part, because Bigotes had earlier insisted that tribes along the way act peacefully toward the Spaniards rather than fight them.

Relations got worse. With winter fast approaching, Coronado sent López de Cárdenas—the man who had discovered the Grand Canyon—to Tiguex to begin establishing a winter camp. López de Cárdenas entered a Tiguex pueblo, ordered all its inhabitants to leave, and moved his men into the houses, where they found plenty of food and warm clothing.

Coronado arrived with even more men. He went from village to village, taking more blankets and warm clothing.

The situation was becoming critical. All it needed was one more incident to light the fuse. That happened when one of Coronado's men entered a village and spotted a pretty Indian woman. He dismounted, ordered a man standing nearby to hold his horse, and pursued the woman. The man holding the horse turned out to be the woman's husband.

Coronado had enough of a sense of fairness to realize that this action was wrong, but he did not know which of his men was the guilty one. He called the husband to come forward and identify the man who had attacked his wife.

"All white men seem the same to me," the husband said. "But I know the horse."

He walked over to the corral and pointed to one of the horses. "That one," he said.

The Spaniard who owned the horse denied any wrongdoing. Coronado refused to convict one of his men on the basis of a horse identification, so he dropped the case.

The Indians didn't. Early the next morning, a group of them crept up to the corral, killed one of the Spaniards' Indian guards, and stole about 30 horses. In retaliation, Coronado ordered López de Cárdenas to attack the raiders' village.

Coronado and his men traveled through the dusty deserts of the southwest hunting for gold and riches. They crossed rivers and trekked through dried lava beds, where the ash left over from volcanoes would blacken their shoes.

López de Cárdenas and his heavily armed men quickly overcame the resistance from the stunned villagers. The frightened men fled for the safety of the kiva, their central place of worship. Most of it was below ground. They may have believed that their gods would protect them. They were wrong.

The Spaniards lit branches on fire and threw them into the kiva. Choking and sputtering, the Indians were forced out into the open and quickly captured. López de Cárdenas pronounced a harsh and brutal sentence on them. Because they had stolen horses, they were to be put to death. Several of them were tied to stakes with brush and sticks piled at the base. At first the villagers didn't realize what was happening. But when the Spaniards lit the piles and the screams of the men began filling the air, their intentions became clear. Some broke free, and even though they had no weapons, tried to fight back. Their hands and feet were no match for the sharp steel of Spanish swords. All 200 of the captives died.

And Coronado wasn't finished. The rest of his men finally appeared, so he had to find shelter, food, and clothing for them. The Spaniards kept swarming into Tiguex villages, taking what they needed and burning the rest. The survivors retreated to a village called Moho, their best constructed town. They hoped they would be safe there.

Coronado wouldn't leave them alone. In the chill of January 1541, he approached and read the *requerimiento* yet another time. Carrying ladders, the soldiers tried to scale the walls. But this time they were beaten back. A few were killed. The Spaniards settled in for a long siege, because they knew there was very little water inside the walls. The Indians tried to dig a well, but it collapsed, killing about 30 people. They did have a brief respite during a heavy snowfall, when they melted the snow and drank it. Eventually, about the middle of March, they were almost out of water and asked for a truce. The women and children passed safely through the Spanish lines. When the men tried to sneak out a few nights later, they were discovered and killed.■

This is a reconstruction of Coronado's campsite built at Kuaua Pueblo (Tiguex) Bernalillo, New Mexico.

This dusty desert in Arizona can get to over 100 degrees during the day, but then gets cold and chilly at night. While Coronado's men hovered around their campfires late at night, they thought of Quivira, which they had heard was one of the richest places on earth. It was really just another Indian village.

THE GREAT PLAINS AND QUIVIRA

Coronado's men had one thought to help keep them warm during the long chilly winter weeks while they kept watch over the besieged Indians at Moho: Quivira. The Turk kept adding to his tales of the riches that were to be found there. Even the poorest people ate off silver plates and drank from golden goblets, he told them. They took naps under trees with golden balls dangling from their branches. The Quiviran king was rowed around on a boat with golden oarlocks. And just beyond Quivira was an even richer land, called Harahey. The Turk didn't tell the Spanish one thing, however. Harahey was the homeland of his people, the Pawnee Indians.

The Spaniards' renewed gold lust made them impatient for the snow to melt. When that finally happened in April, Coronado left Tiguex and headed east.

Coronado and his men soon reached the southern end of the Great Plains and saw great herds of buffalo. They were amazed by the huge flat spread of the country, without hills, mountains, or forests. They called it the Llano Estacado, or "staked plains," because they felt that without driving stakes into the otherwise featureless terrain, they would become lost.

In a way, they already were lost. They had been heading southeast ever since leaving Tiguex, and Quivira lay to the northeast. Finally, the plains gave way to steep cliffs. There they met Indians known as Teyas, from whom they learned that Quivira lay far to the north, nowhere near the route they had been taking. And they described the city in a far different way than the Turk's glowing portrayal.

Late in May, 600 miles and five weeks after they had left, Coronado sent most of his men back to Tiguex. He took 30 horsemen and a dozen foot soldiers up through the Texas Panhandle, through Oklahoma and into Kansas. He brought the Turk with him, in chains. A month later he reached the banks of the Arkansas River, where he soon met some Indians who claimed to be from Quivira. When Coronado eagerly questioned them about the gold in their land, they were confused. They had no idea what he was talking about. They didn't even know what gold was.

Coronado angrily confronted the Turk. Soon the Turk confessed that he had lied. All along he had been in a conspiracy with Bigotes to exhaust the Spaniards and weaken their horses. Without horses, they could be killed and the Indian lands would no longer be in danger.

Nevertheless, Coronado wanted to see Quivira for himself, so he pushed on. Seeing the actual village was still a shock. It was simply some grass huts near a river. Despite their disappointment, Coronado and his men were impressed with the richness of the land itself.

One of them, Juan Jaramillo, wrote, "This country has a fine appearance, the like of which I have never seen anywhere in our Spain. . . . I am of the belief that it will be very productive for all sorts of commodities."

More than 450 years later, his words have proved to be accurate. The land they were exploring lies in the heart of the Wheat Belt, which produces enough grain every year to feed millions of people throughout the world.

Coronado stayed in Quivira for a month, sending his men out on scouting expeditions. Some may have traveled as far as Nebraska. All told, they had marched more than 3,000 miles since setting out more than a year before.

Coronado noticed that the Quivirans, who had been friendly when he arrived, were becoming more hostile. He soon learned that the Turk, not content with having lied to him about the existence of gold and then trying to get them hopelessly lost in the Great Plains, was telling the Quivirans that the Spaniards were evil spirits and should be killed. Coronado couldn't take any more deceit from him. He ordered one of his men to come up behind the Turk with a rope and strangle him.

Fearing the onset of winter, Coronado decided to rejoin the rest of his men in Tiguex. Unlike the war and killings the previous winter, this time there was relative peace between the Spaniards and the Indians, though it is doubtful that the Indians enjoyed the company of their "guests." To help pass the time, the men exercised their horses. One day Coronado joined them. He challenged one of his officers to a race.

Coronado was riding at full speed when the rotted leather strap securing his saddle to the horse broke. Coronado fell to the ground and his horse kicked him in the head. He lay unconscious for several days. When he came to, he told his anxious men about a prophecy he had had before he left Spain. An astrologer, a person who believed that someone's fate could be predicted by carefully studying the stars and planets, had told him that he would become a large landowner in a new country far from his native Spain. But he would also die as the result of a bad fall.

As he recovered, his mood changed. Previously he had talked as if he were in favor of spending another year looking for gold. But now all he wanted to do was go back home. He missed his wife and his home.

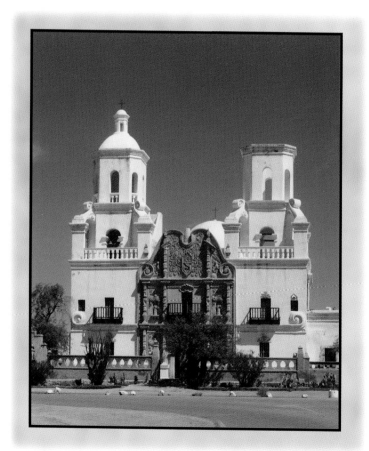

In the 1500s, the king of Spain declared that all the natives in the New World would be converted to Christianity. The Indians were forced to give up their tribal religions and worship God as Christians. The San Xavier Mission School, shown here, was one of many missions set up by the Spanish to teach Christianity.

Even though they hadn't found any gold in almost two years, several of his officers wanted to continue the expedition. They wanted to go back to Quivira and even beyond to see if they could find the golden cities. They argued over and over with him, but they couldn't change his mind. In April 1542, Coronado and his men headed back to Mexico. Three of the priests, who weren't under Coronado's direct orders, decided to stay behind and try to convert the Indians to Christianity. All three were eventually killed.

The trip back was uneventful. The men were gloomy. As they got closer to Mexico City, many of them began to desert. They feared that they would be punished for some of the things they had done to the Indians. As a result, Coronado came back to Mexico City with less than 100 of the men who had originally set out with him. They had covered more than 6,000 miles and discovered many natural wonders. But because they returned without gold, they were regarded as failures. ■

These are the ruins of Kuaua Pueblo at Coronado State monument.
These particular ruins are believed to be the site of Hawikuh, the
city sought by Coronado in 1540.

A HIGH WATER MARK IN HISTORY

At first, Coronado's life seemed to return to normal. He resumed his duties as governor of New Galicia and settled down with his family, which now included two daughters.

But soon Spanish officials began investigating some of the things that had happened during the expedition. Don García López de Cárdenas, the man who had burned Indians at the stake, had to go back to Spain to stand trial in 1544. He claimed that everything he had done was in the "heat of battle" and was therefore acceptable. The court disagreed, and he spent seven years in jail.

Coronado himself wasn't above suspicion. A special judge who came from Spain the following year charged Coronado with committing "great cruelties upon the natives of the land through which he passed." Coronado was removed from the governorship of New Galicia and brought to Mexico City to stand trial. Unlike López de Cárdenas, he was found innocent.

However, the scandals connected with the expedition and the fact that he had come home empty-handed ruined his reputation. Though Mendoza gave him several positions in the government of the city and he maintained a reputation for being efficient in the performance of his duties, it was clear that Coronado was no longer destined to achieve great things. Even though he was only 32, an age when most people are just beginning long, successful careers, Coronado's one-time bright future had dimmed.

Another reason for his decline may have been that he never fully regained his health. Many people believed that the astrologer's prediction was correct, that being kicked by his horse after his fall hastened his death. He died in 1554, 12 years after returning.

Apparently the date was about September 22. Mexico City's public records for the end of September in that year say that he didn't show up for a meeting because he had died only a few days previously. He was 44 years old.

No one had realized it at the time, but the great age of Spanish exploration was at its peak when Coronado's exhausted men staggered back to Mexico City. The year 1542 turned out to be perhaps the greatest single year in the history of exploration. Besides marking the end of Coronado's expedition, several other significant events occurred that year.

• Hernando de Soto, who died of a fever, was buried in the Mississippi River after exploring most of the great American southeast.

• Ships under the command of Juan Cabrillo explored the West Coast as far north as Oregon.

• Ruy Lopez de Villalobos pioneered a route from Mexico across the Pacific Ocean to the Philippine Islands that galleons heavily laden with treasure would continue to follow for decades.

• After having climbed to the tops of the Andes mountains, Francisco de Orellana finished a two-year raft trip down the Amazon River to the Atlantic Ocean.

• Álvar Cabeza de Vaca—the same man who had survived eight years in the American wilderness—finished a thousand-mile hike across the grassy plains of southern Brazil.

In almost exactly 50 years, Spain had acquired an overseas empire the size of the Roman Empire. For nearly another half century, the Spanish consolidated their gains and remained the leading world power.

By then, Francisco Coronado had slipped into obscurity. No one even knew where he was buried until well into the 20th century. And until recently, few people knew his story.

That isn't surprising, because for many years the accomplishments of almost all the courageous Spanish explorers of the early 16th century were not given the full recognition they deserved.

There are several reasons for this. In 1517, two years before Cortés landed in Mexico, Martin Luther nailed his famous 95 theses to the door of a church in Germany and began the Protestant Reformation. Not long after Coronado died, Henry VIII of England broke off from the Catholic Church to form the Church of England. And in 1588 the English prevented an invasion by the Spanish Armada. That ended a century of Spanish military dominance and began the rise of England as a major world power.

Many people outside of Spain were jealous of Spain and what its explorers had accomplished. And as the division between Catholics and Protestants became wider, the believers on each side disliked each other more and more.

In particular, the Reverend Richard Hakluyt, an English geographer, wrote several histories that changed dates and distorted facts to give the impression that England had been just as important, if not more so, in the discovery and colonization of the New World than Spain had been. In other words, there was a systematic effort to downplay what Spain had accomplished. Nearly all of the 13 colonies were founded by the English, so when the United States declared its independence from England, this tendency to overrate the English contribution and underrate what the Spanish had done naturally continued.

Yet it is a fact that as the 17th century began, there was not a single English colony anywhere on the American continent. There were, however, hundreds of Spanish colonies. Explorers such as Coronado, Cortés, and de Soto and their men were speaking Spanish in many areas of this country decades, even centuries, before anyone heard a single word of English.

Today, you can visit the Coronado National Monument in southeast Arizona, which is located where many historians believe that Coronado crossed into what is now the United States. Nearly all the land there is in the same condition it was in when Coronado and his men arrived there more than 450 years ago.

If you close your eyes and let your imagination wander, you can almost hear the creaking of the leather saddles on the horses, the clink of metal stirrups, and the quiet conversations of the infantrymen who were walking next to each other.

Coronado may have been chasing a chimera. But he found something else: immortality.■

CHRONOLOGY

TIMELINE IN HISTORY

TIMELINE IN HISTORY

1521   Ferdinand Magellan is killed in the Philippine Islands; his surviving crew members eventually complete the first voyage around the world

1524   Giovanni da Verrazano explores Atlantic coast from North Carolina to Maine on behalf of France

1526   Esteban Gomez establishes but soon abandons settlement on the Savannah River (present-day Georgia)

1528   Pánfilo de Narváez explores Gulf coast from Florida to Texas, but his expedition is wrecked

1531   Francisco Pizarro begins conquest of Peru

1534   Jacques Cartier begins exploring the St. Lawrence River for France

1539   Hernando de Soto leaves Cuba to begin exploration of southeast of present-day USA; eventually discovers Mississippi River

1540   Francisco Vásquez de Coronado begins exploration that eventually extends as far as modern-day Kansas

1542   Juan Rodriguez Cabrillo and Bartolome Ferrelo explore west coast of North America as far north of Oregon

1551   Real y Pontificia Universidad de Mexico becomes first university on the North American continent

1565   Pedro Menéndez de Aviles establishes St. Augustine, Florida, which becomes oldest US city.

1607   Jamestown colony founded

1620   Pilgrims land at Plymouth Rock

FOR FURTHER READING

De Castañeda, Pedro. *The Journey of Coronado*. Mineola, NY: Dover Books, 1990.

Crisfield, Deborah. *The Travels of Francisco de Coronado*. Austin, TX: Raintree Steck-Vaughn, 2001.

Jensen, Malcolm C. *Francisco Coronado*. New York: Franklin Watts, Inc., 1974.

Lavender, David. *Desoto, Coronado, Cabrillo: Explorers of the Northern Mystery*. Washington, DC: US Government Printing Office, 1992.

Marcovitz, Hal. *Francisco Coronado and the Exploration of the American Southwest*. Philadelphia: Chelsea House Publishers, 2000.

Nardo, Don. *Francisco Coronado*. New York: Franklin Watts, Inc., 2002.

Preston, Douglas. *Cities of Gold*. New York: Simon & Schuster, 1992.

Stein, R. Conrad. *The World's Great Explorers: Francisco de Coronado*. Chicago: Children's Press, 1992.

Udall, Stewart L. *To the Inland Empire: Coronado and Our Spanish Legacy*. New York: Doubleday and Company, 1987.

Time-Life Books (eds.). *The Spanish West*. New York: Time-Life, 1976.

Weisberg, Barbara. *Coronado's Golden Quest*. Austin, TX: Raintree Steck-Vaughn, 1992.

ON THE WEB

PBS - THE WEST - The Journey of Coronado
www.pbs.org/weta/thewest/resources/archives/one/corona1.htm
Hispanic colonization of North America
http://www.rose-hulman.edu/~delacova/colonization.htm
Francisco Coronado
http://cybersleuth-kids.com/sleuth/History/Explorers
Francisco_Coronado/
Hispanic Timeline
www.getnet.com/~1stbooks/chron3.htm
Spain in Arizona (good coronado links)
http://coe.west.asu.edu/students/lleavitt/spanish.htm

GLOSSARY

astrologer (a-STRAWL-uh-jer): person who makes predictions about future events by studying the stars and planets

Aztec (AS-tek): advanced civilization that controlled Mexico for several centuries

bishop (BISH-up): a high-ranking Christian church leader

casualties (KAZH-oo-al-tees): people who are killed or wounded as the result of a fight or accident

chasm (KAZ-um): a deep crack or narrow gorge in the earth's surface

chimera (kai-MERE-uh): imaginary animal with a lion's head, a goat's body and a snake's tail that spits fire like a dragon; something imaginary, an illusion

coat of mail: flexible armor made of interlocking metal rings

competent (KOM-puh-tent): very capable, qualified, skillful

congregation (kong-gruh-GA-shun): group of people who meet regularly for worship

conquistadores (cone-KEES-ta-door-ees): Spanish soldiers who conquered vast territories in the New World crossbow: weapon in which a bow is placed crosswise on a heavy wooden stock. It shoots a short arrow with great force

cuirass (kwi-RACE): a metal vest to protect the chest

devoid (dee-VOYD): empty, containing nothing

friar (FRY-ur): a member of a religious group who chooses to live in poverty and spread the word of God

gourd (GORD): hollowed-out shell of some types of fruit, sometimes believed to have magical powers

Inca (INK-uh): civilization that controlled part of South America

intrepid (in-TRE-pid): brave, daring

legacy (LEG-uh-see): something handed down from the past

malign (muh-LINE): evil, producing suffering

mentor (MEN-tor): an older person who acts as a guide and advisor to a younger person

motto (MAH-toe): a brief phrase or sentence that expresses a guiding principle or goal

musket: an early form of the rifle

optimism (AWP-tim-izm): belief that events will turn out in the best possible way

prophecy (PRAWF-uh-see): a prediction of the future

remote (ree-MOTE): far away, distant

siege (SEEJ): surrounding and blockading a fort or town to force the inhabitants to surrender when they run out of food and water

truce (TROOS): A temporary halt in fighting

INDEX